Workbook

WHEN THE HEAD HURTS

*How The Emotional Health of Leaders Impacts
Everything & Everyone They Lead*

DR. KHAALIDA FORBES

KEEN VISION
PUBLISHING

THIS SAFE SPACE BELONGS TO:

_____

WHAT'S INSIDE

RULES OF
ENGAGEMENT

❙ TAKE DEEP BREATHS...OFTEN!

A question or conversation hits a sensitive spot? Don't run. Breathe through it. Cry through it if you must, but keep healing forward.

❙ BE HONEST WITH GOD & YOURSELF

Facing painful truths about ourselves can be challenging, but you can't heal what you refuse to reveal. In this safe space, honesty is always the best policy.

❙ COMMIT TO THE WORK

If you're working through these pages alone or with a group, dedicate a block of time to DOING THE WORK. Move at your own pace, but don't let your healing process grow cold. Stay the course!

❙ READ THE BOOK BEFORE YOUR SESSION

Imagine that this workbook is your personal therapist. Would you show up to your session without completing your homework? *When The Head Hurts* (The Book) is your companion (and homework) for each session. The insight in the chapters will aid you as you journey through this workbook.

TAKE
a deep
BREATH

Let's
BEGIN. . .

INTRODUCTION

It's not by happenstance that you find yourself starting this workbook either with yourself or with a trusted group. You've been led to this journey because you are a leader, and we know that leaders are, if nothing else, givers. You are always giving of your knowledge, gifts, talents, time, care, resources, energy, and finances. You are expected to always be available to pour, guide, and direct. As a leader, you must be able to oversee what is happening now, while simultaneously projecting into the future, and returning to the present, all in order to provide people with the steps needed to journey to what lies ahead. What a dance.

God orchestrated you to this journey of emotional wellness, in this season of your life, because God wants to talk to you. Down through the years, you have counseled, supported, and encouraged countless people through their seasons of hurt and pain. Don't you deserve to pause and give attention to your own hurts? Yes, the organization is important. But so are you. The truth of the matter is, the organization you lead can go no further than your level of internal wellness. If you want to take your organization to higher heights, if you want to have the influence God has called you to have in the earth, you must believe that you deserve the care you've given others.

The goal of this workbook is to offer you a more in-depth guide to processing through many of the points that were highlighted in my book "When The Head Hurts" (which I suggest that you read before or along with this workbook). This workbook is your opportunity to stop, assess, breathe, and heal. My prayer is that this will be God's way of reaching out to you in your internal distress. God has seen what you've experienced, and God has heard your cries. Let God use this workbook in this season as one of many tools to rescue you from your emotional Egypt, so that God can bring you into a season of peace, stability, and overflowing joy.

Let's pray.....

Eternal God,

I pray for every person whom you have divinely orchestrated to be reading this book. You are the author of these pages because you desire to speak to your children. You want them to know that regardless of how big they've become, they're still your child. Father, you know every story, every incident, every misuse and abuse. You know when it happened, where it happened, and how long it lasted. You know every internal emotional fracture and every broken place within them. All I humbly ask of you is that you reveal to each reader the importance of their past's impact on their present and future. Allow this to be a sacred season wherein they can truly see the need for healing. From this book, guide each one toward the genesis of a healing journey that is tailor made just for them. Allow this book to simply be the seed that opens their mind, heart, and spirit to their need to receive your healing balm. Lastly, heal those whom our hurts have wounded, and ultimately usher us all into the beauty, peace, and strength that comes from the fountain of holy wellness.

In Jesus' Name, Amen, It Is So.

I I I I I I

What Are Your Symptoms?

Leader, understand that pain manifests in various ways. I want us to begin this journey with you exploring the various symptoms that you may have been ignoring.

SYMPTOMS *a physical or mental feature which is regarded as indicating a condition of dis-ease.*

In the last 3 to 5 years, what emotional experiences have you had that could by symptoms of a greater emotional trauma (e.g., difficulty sleeping, lack of motivation, un-identified anger.)

_____   _____
_____   _____
_____   _____
_____   _____

May I humbly suggest that you're not angry, you're hurting. You're not frustrated, you're hurting. You're not defensive, you're hurting. You're not controlling, you're hurting. You're not manipulative, you're just hurting.

Every trauma you've experienced, every disappointment, every verbal, emotional, physical, sexual, and spiritual misuse and abuse, all the lies told about you, each person that left when they promised to stay, from birth up to the very moment you find yourself reading this book, it all hurt you in ways that you haven't allowed yourself to be consciously aware of. But the truth is, you were hurt, and most likely you're still hurting. You never really got the examination, diagnostic, and prescription that you needed and deserved. You've never been able to be the patient, and for that, I am deeply sorry. But I do have good news for you...

The Doctor will see you now.

Right before you take the next step within this workbook I have an important question for you to ponder. This question lies within the 5th chapter of John.

BIBLE STUDY: THE QUESTION

Some time later, Jesus went up to Jerusalem for one of the Jewish festivals. Now there is in Jerusalem near the Sheep Gate a pool, which in Aramaic is called Bethesda and which is surrounded by five covered colonnades. Here a great number of disabled people used to lie—the blind, the lame, the paralyzed. One who was there had been an invalid for thirty-eight years. When Jesus saw him lying there and learned that he had been in this condition for a long time, he asked him, "Do you want to get well?"

JOHN 5:1-5

Jesus poses the question, "Do you want to be made well?" To the naked eye, Jesus' question could be seen as insensitive. Of course the man wanted to be made well. Honestly, who would want to spend the rest of their life ill? Jesus didn't ask this question to offend the man. I believe Jesus' intent was to invite him to evaluate his emotional state and it's impact on his ability to truly have the faith and subsequent tenacity for wellness. Jesus wanted the lame man to take accountability for his wholeness.

1. Why did the lame man give Jesus excuses at to why he couldn't get well?

2. What excuses have you given to Jesus as to why you, yourself, have yet to get emotionally well?

We can spend so many years in unwell states, that we become accustomed to it. We find ways to make the uncomfortable comfortable.

3. What has your emotionally blindness kept you from seeing?

4. How has your emotional lameness prevented you from forward progression?

5. How has your emotional paralysis stagnated your very participation in life?

6. Just like the lame man, many of you have TRIED! But there has been a missing link that has kept you in perpetual cycles. What behaviors have kept you bound in emotionally unhealthy cycles? (e.g., unforgiveness, addiction, people pleasing)

COUCH
Conversations

The current climate of the church finds itself in the middle of an internal audit. The very things we thought were hidden (situations, struggles, sins, and strongholds; proclivities, passions, perversions, and pride; desires, diseases, dysfunctions, and demons) have now been laid bare before us all. For years, we have endeavored to clean the mess by placing great emphasis on the congregation's mental, emotional, and spiritual well-being. We are finally at the point of accepting the difficult reality that many of the church's current crises do not necessarily stem from the pew *but from the pulpit*.

The purpose of this session was to help you identify the symptoms that point to your emotional unwellness. In this session's Couch Conversations, you will explore how your emotional wellbeing has impacted your ability to live and lead. Once you are complete, reflect over your answers and imagine what your life would be like if you were MADE WHOLE.

1. How much is your current emotional handicap impacting you?

2. How much energy have you put into conforming your life to your emotional ailments? How much time have you lost to date?

3. What opportunities have you missed simply because you reduced your life to your trauma effects?

4. Do you want to be WHOLE?

| | | | | | |

SESSION ONE

TOP 3 TAKE-AWAYS

TAKE *a deep* BREATH

SESSION TWO

Disrobing

The year 2013 started with an alarming number of senior leaders committing suicide. After many of these tragedies were mourned, it was later revealed that these leaders suffered silently with mental and emotional health concerns. How painful is it to realize that someone who stood behind the sacred desk, week in and week out, encouraging, uplifting, and declaring life over bowed heads and broken hearts, secretly battled seeing value in their own life?

Though you may have never considered suicide, for years, many of you reading this book have worn the very same mask. You know the one I'm referring to. It's the face of excitement you put on, though you barely got rest the night before, because you spent hours wrestling with trauma flashbacks. It's the poker face you put on when you walk through the sanctuary doors, even though you just had a serious argument with your spouse moments earlier and are still emotionally flustered. It's the face of joy you wear even though you just got the most unpleasant text message from a family member moments before you entered the meeting.

Despite what has happened throughout the week, when it is time to stand before the people, leaders across the world reach into their bag and pull out their good and faithful mask that allows them to hide the horrors, cover the casualties, and disguise the disappointments. It's the mask that makes everyone else feel safe, secure, and supported except for the wearer.

1. Do you wear a mask?

2. Why do you wear a mask?

3. Where do you wear a mask? What masks do you tend to wear in those spaces and why?

Everyone's masks look different depending on what they are trying to cover up, who they are trying to hide the truth from, and the platform they desire to obtain or maintain. I want to ask a couple of questions that can solidify if you are in fact wearing a mask...

4. What ways do you avoid God by serving God?

5. Are you open to embracing positive emotions, but flee from negative feelings that surface? What physical or emotional signs come up within you when you're faced with negative feelings?

6. What areas of your life have you refused to pray about? Why?

7. What distinct differences have you seen between how you conduct yourself in your role, versus how you show up in your being? (e.g., do you employ different personalities based on different contexts?)

8. What areas of your life do you find it most challenging to erect and maintain boundaries?

BIBLE STUDY: WHAT ABOUT YOUR LOG?

Do not judge and criticize and condemn [others unfairly with an attitude of self-righteous superiority as though assuming the office of a judge], so that you will not be judged [unfairly]. For just as you [hypocritically] judge others [when you are sinful and unrepentant], so will you be judged; and in accordance with your standard of measure [used to pass out judgment], judgment will be measured to you. Why do you look at the [insignificant] speck that is in your brother's eye, but do not notice and acknowledge the [egregious] log that is in your own eye? Or how can you say to your brother, 'Let me get the speck out of your eye,' when there is a log in your own eye? You hypocrite (play-actor, pretender), first get the log out of your own eye, and then you will see clearly to take the speck out of your brother's eye.

MATTHEW 7:1-5

Because they have worn their mask for so long, many leaders have convinced themselves that there is absolutely nothing wrong with them. What if I told you that because you can't see yourself, *you also can't see the people God has called you to lead?* It's possible that the revelation you've been receiving from God wasn't for the people but intended for you. It's possible that there aren't as many issues on your staff as you believe there are, but your compromised sight is magnifying the minor and minimizing the major. It's possible that you keep seeing problems in others because you aren't seeing the problems within yourself. It's possible that your last sermon series wasn't a big hit with the church because you were preaching to yourself and not them.

1. Have you been strongly judging others in certain areas as an unconscious attempt to ignore it in yourself? (If so, in what areas?)

2. Have you been counseling others in areas that you've been personally ignoring? What are your thoughts as you think about the counsel you've provided them?

3. What obstacles do you feel you'd have to overcome in order to address the plank in your own eye?

WHY YOU WEAR THE MASK

REPRESSION - A thought, feeling, or emotion that is NOT expressed.

Very often, when one suffers from repression, they deny that thoughts, feelings, or emotions even exists. To repress means to hide, and it is used as a defense mechanism believed to provide protection. Repression may temporarily keep the issues out of the spotlight, but the impact could destroy your life and the lives of those connected to you. Leader, I know that you believed that wearing the mask would protect you from unwanted publicity. However, it is more dangerous than you know.

Being unaware of our emotions prevents us from recognizing how they could be affecting and harming ourselves and others. Repression distorts our observations of the moment, memories of the past, and expectations of the future. In fact, repression is the culprit behind addiction, abuse, depression, ulcers, stomach, colon, breast cancer, and a plethora of other physical, emotional, and mental dysfunctions. In addition to being afraid of negative spotlights, there are many reasons why individuals choose to repress their thoughts, feelings, and emotions.

1. What communities do you fear being rejected from if your imperfections become visible?

2. What traumas are you afraid to revisit, even if revisiting is the pathway to healing?

3. What messages have you received through society that have caused you to fear authenticity?

4. What messages have you received ministerially that have caused you to fear authenticity?

5. How do ministry communities perceive those who struggle with what you struggle with?

6. Have your answers to question #5 contributed to your discomfort in removing your mask?

COUCH *Conversations*

Asking you to remove the mask feels like you're being required to remove your safety net. I understand that the invitation this book is extending to you seems like it will do more harm to your life than good. However, it is quite the contrary. **The enemy wants you to remain in the dark so that light can never hit those painful areas of your life.** He wants you to believe that removing the mask will leave you alone, desperate, and embarrassed. Make no mistake: I completely understand what this chapter asks you to do. Difficult things are easier said than done. I understand that the fear of judgment, facing the truth, reliving the past, and potentially being ridiculed by society and the church are large pills to swallow. However, I challenge you to move beyond your fear of temporary backlash and finally remove your mask. If you can make it through this session, the others won't be nearly as difficult. If you reconcile to remove the mask, the journey to true freedom will begin.

1. Can you visualize a life in which you are not weighed down by fear of exposure because you're showing up whole? What does that look like?

2. Can you see yourself authentically leading people to healthier lifestyles because you did the internal work to resolve your past, and are now employing healthy strategies of daily wellness? What does that look like?

3. What would your personal life look like if you could wake up every morning free?

| | | | | | |

TOP 3 TAKE-AWAYS

TAKE

a deep

BREATH

Stay In Your Lane

By now, you've learned that the health of your organization relies heavily upon your emotional well-being. However, as you have taken a look at the symptoms that point to your lack of emotional wholeness, you might be wondering, "How on earth did I get here?" In this session, we will explore the culprits of your current emotional condition with the hope that as you pinpoint the root, you will walk away from unhealthy practices and cultural beliefs that keep you unwell.

To put it plainly, Leader, a large reason why you may struggle to remove the mask and take the time away from ministry to rest, receive counsel, and experience a healthy life, is because you don't understand the role.

1. Why do you feel it's a challenge to take a break from your church?

2. What signs have led you to believe that your church can't survive in your absence? Or, is that truthfully not actually the case?

Think back to when you first understood the role of a senior leader in the church. If you grew up in church, it was probably as a child. If you started attending church later in life, it might have been when you were new to the faith.

3. How did you see the role of senior leaders?

4. What did you believe they should be doing?

5. How did your understanding of a senior leaders' role shift when you went from a pew view to a pulpit view?

Many of you are struggling to accept the truth about your actual role because, for so many years, this is what you were taught to do in order to be a "good pastor." However, when you stick to the true role and assignment, congregants will feel that they have a good healthy pastor. Just think about it, how much time are you really spending in consecration throughout the week if you are at every social gathering your congregants host? Some interaction that congregants may desire from senior leaders, actually takes the senior leader away from their actual spiritual responsibilities to the church.

1. What responsibilities could you delegate to other leaders in the ministry?

2. What creative steps can you take to educate the congregation on your role?

BIBLE STUDY: IS THAT REALLY YOUR JOB?

Christ is the head of the church: and he is the savior of the body.

EPHESIANS 5:23b

If you are still struggling to comprehend why you must set healthy boundaries between yourself and congregants, it's possible that you could be battling with what is known as a Savior Complex.

1. What do you believe is God's responsibility to congregants and your responsibility to congregants? Do you believe there are responsibilities that overlap? Use the Venn Diagram below to record your response.

RESPONSIBILITIES TO SHEEP/CONGREGANTS

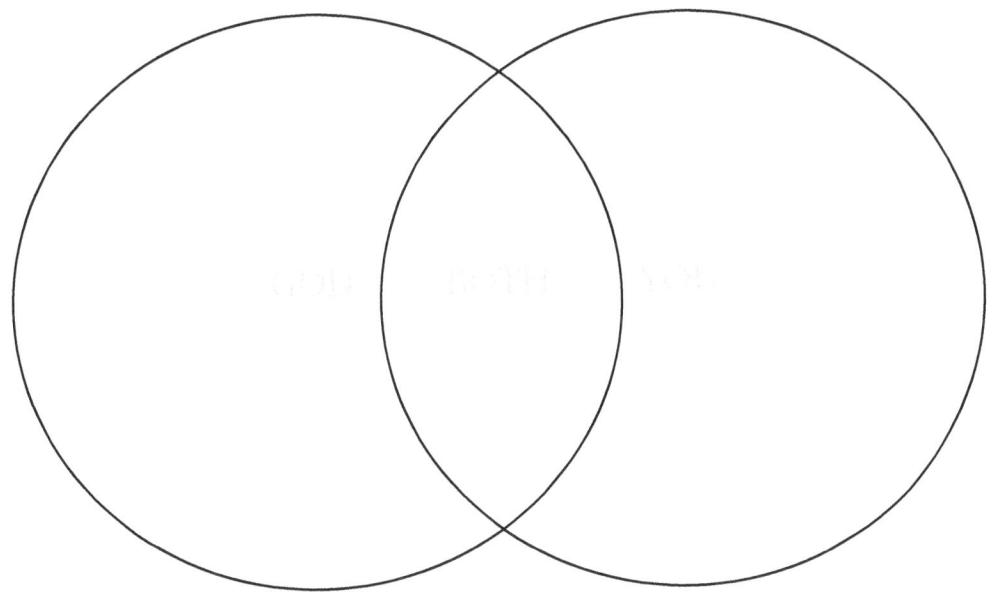

2. In what ways have you taken on more responsibility as Pastor than scripture demands?

3. Describe past seasons where you've felt a need to "save" a member(s) only to later realize that what was most needed was them turning fully to Christ?

4. In what ways does "saving others" satisfy your own needs? How do you feel after you have "come to the rescue?"

5. In what other ways and contexts can you satisfy the above needs?

6. What is the top obstacle to you putting your emotional health first?

7. What concerns do you have about being less hands on as a leader?

COUCH
Conversations

Until we are honest and establish healthy boundaries between the pulpit and the pew, the church will remain unhealthy. Realizing that there could be an unhealthy dynamic between you and the congregation can be difficult, but rest assured that there are things you can do to begin to turn the situation around. Yes, there may be disappointment in the culture due to unmet expectations that were never communicated or agreed to. However, as the leader, you must have the courage to reframe dynamics, restructure access, and redefine roles and expectations – despite the kickback you may receive. Will there be some people who reject a healthier pastor? Yes! Will there be some people who reject a healthier community? Possibly. However, have the courage to make the turn for yourself and for your congregation's health. Eventually, your courage may cause them to lean in with interest, and they will end up coming on the ride as well.

1. Starting today what can you incorporate into your life that may require less time at the church but more time for your health?

2. If time was no concern, and money was no object, what would you do to restore yourself regularly?

SESSION THREE

TOP 3 TAKE-AWAYS

TAKE
a deep
BREATH

SESSION FOUR

Say Baaaa . . .

A shepherd guides sheep daily and ensures that they each are covered and protected. The shepherd knows each sheep intimately, so he is aware if a sheep is missing. A shepherd puts oil on the head of sheep to ensure they don't bash their heads trying to rid themselves of gnats and other flying pests. A shepherd knows when the water may be too high and weigh sheep down. But there is a greater shepherd that was the originator of shepherding. This shepherd is mighty and powerful, our Lord, our savior, our King.

1. In what ways have you minimized allowing yourself to be known by God intimately?

2. Provide examples of how working "FOR GOD" may be causing you to forfeit intimacy "WITH GOD?"

3. Since you've become a Sr. Leader is the Lord still YOUR Shepherd?

Herein lies the schizophrenic dynamic of the clergy position. We are called upon by God to wear two hats. We are both shepherd and sheep. We cannot escape our sheep-ness. For even when we function in the role and the anointing of being a shepherd, there's something about my sheep-ness that is hard to contain. My sheep-ness is so unpredictable that I can't manage it myself. I'm a shepherd of sheep, but yet I'm a sheep that needs a shepherd.

BISHOP ULMAR

For many of you, the above quote from Bishop Ulmar brought about a sense of relief, a reminder that as you carry the weight of being the senior pastor, you are not carrying it alone. Just as you shepherd the people, you, too, have a shepherd to lean to and run to in times of need. What is critical for clergy leadership to remember and daily embrace is that you are NOT your own Shepherd! Furthermore, when it comes to the members of the local body you serve, You are not THE Shepherd; you are an UNDERshepherd.

1. How do you view sheep?

2. Did you believe that your elevation in ministry meant that you graduated out of your role as one of God's sheep?

3. What occurrences in your life become clear reminders that you are still in-fact a sheep?

4. What daily spiritual or natural disciplines would assist you in being reminded that though you under shepherd, you are still God's sheep? (e.g., daily devotion time, scripture reading for intimacy, not sermon preparation...)

Many people who enter our churches on Sunday mornings have been let down and disillusioned by what's occurring in the world. As a result, they desperately need something to believe in. Very often, it is hard to place their hope solely in an invisible God. Therefore, they place this hope in the senior leader, who they can physically see. Sometimes this is done consciously, but often it's done unconsciously. When congregants see their leader operate in anointed teaching and preaching, prophecy, or be used by God as a conduit to administrate miracles, signs, and wonders, they are in awe of the anointing. Many develop a reverence, not just for God, who empowered the leader, but also for the leader themselves.

1. How is your church more leader-focused than God-focused?

2. Is grace expected for the congregation only, or is leadership given grace for growth? If not, what do you believe has attributed to this?

3. What ways have you felt pressured to be perfect?

4. What areas do you feel the majority of that pressure coming from?

5. Have you carried perceptions that those who occupy your current role should be perfect?

6. Leader, if the people's pressure/unrealistic expectations are causing you to hide your issues, and your issues are making you hide from God. Are you truly availing yourself for the Shepherd to lead you to wholeness?

BIBLE STUDY: CHILDISH

At that time the disciples came to Jesus and asked, "Who is greatest in the kingdom of heaven?" He called a little child and set him before them, and said, "I assure you and most solemnly say to you, unless you repent [that is, change your inner self—your old way of thinking, live changed lives] and become like children [trusting, humble, and forgiving], you will never enter the kingdom of heaven. Therefore, whoever humbles himself like this child is greatest in the kingdom of heaven.

MATTHEW 18:1-3

I know you're an Apostle, but you're still one of God's children. I know you're a Prophet, but you're still one of God's children. I know you're a Pastor, but you're still one of God's children. I know you're an Evangelist, but you're still one of God's children. When was the last time you allowed yourself to crawl into the Father's lap? The consolation, strength, guidance, and healing you need for the next leg of your journey is awaiting you in your Father's loving arms.

1. What are some of the reasons why the disciples inquired about who was the greatest?

2. Why would Jesus ask grown, adult men to become like children?

3. Have you gotten too old for your role?

4. Without realizing it, in what ways has your humility diminished as God has elevated you?

5. I know you are a leader, but are you willing to still be led?

COUCH
Conversations

Every pastor needs a pastor! It's okay to need support as you support others. It doesn't make you weak; it makes you stronger. Having a covering doesn't take away from you. Rather, it adds to you. It can lengthen your cords, add quality to your leadership, and expand your reach. Most things last a little longer when, instead of being laid bare, instead of being left exposed, it's COVERED! But not just any covering. You don't need a placeholder, someone to just verbally claim as your covering, or someone to just visually place on a graphic for the optics. You also don't need a covering that is spiritually deaf or blind. You need a covering that can see God, that knows that God sees them, and they can see you… all of you.

1. What positive experiences have you had with leadership accountability?

2. What negative experiences have you had with leadership accountability?

3. How have those negative experiences caused you to shy away from experiencing the covenant of covering?

4. Provide some examples of past times when a decision you made could have benefitted from the insight of a wise eye?

5. Do you see coverings as guardrails or restrictive restraints? Why?

‖‖‖‖‖‖

SESSION FOUR

TOP 3 TAKE-AWAYS

TAKE
a deep
BREATH

SESSION FIVE

The Scalpel

As we are currently immersed in times that seem to encourage leaders to seek self-advancement above others and prosperity at all costs, prophetic voices are much needed. A prophetic voice carries within itself a sustainable and transformative element. Jesus' ministry was nothing short of prophetic. He was, in fact, the walking embodiment of the prophetic. Although his message was one of love, hope, and salvation, it was also one of discipline, accountability, and kingdom responsibility.

Prophetic voices are charged with speaking truth to power. They have a unique ability to compel those in positions of power to see what could be hidden from their view, and offer them support in having the courage to make a change for the better. The thought of examining our emotions, confronting past hurts, and connecting our internal feelings to our external choices can be a daunting task. A prophetic voice can masterfully utilize a spiritual scalpel to cut and uncover with precision and great care. They do this not to harm, but to help. Prophetic preaching, teaching, and counsel, presents what is truth without fear, and opens up the gates for revelation, introspection, and transformation to occur.

1. What positive experiences have you had with prophetic encounters?

2. What negative experiences had you had with prophetic encounters?

3. How can prophetic engagement benefit you in this season of your leadership?

BIBLE STUDY: YOU ARE THE MAN!

And the Lord sent Nathan [the prophet] to David. He came and said to him, "There were two men in a city, one rich and the other poor. The rich man had a very large number of flocks and herds, But the poor man had nothing but one little ewe lamb which he had purchased and nourished; And it grew up together with him and his children. It ate his food, drank from his cup, it lay in his arms, And was like a daughter to him. Now a traveler (visitor) came to the rich man, And to avoid taking one from his own flock or herd To prepare [a meal] for the traveler who had come to him, He took the poor man's ewe lamb and prepared it for his guest." Then David's anger burned intensely against the man, and he said to Nathan, "As the Lord lives, the man who has done this deserves to die. He shall make restitution for the ewe lamb four times as much [as the lamb was worth], because he did this thing and had no compassion." Then Nathan said to David, "You are the man! Thus says the Lord, the God of Israel, "I anointed you as king over Israel, and I spared you from the hand of Saul."

2 SAMUEL 12:1-7

The hurdle of confronting emotional challenges is admitting that the challenge exists. Simply, you cannot fix what you refuse to face. Leader, prophetic encounters can assist you in realizing that in a certain season, "*You are the man/woman.*" Leader, before you can stand to speak truth to power, you must be on the hearing end of some truths. Despite the uncomfortable feelings the prophetic voice may ignite, the hope is that it will inevitably provoke a transformation from prideful positioning to humble servitude. Leader, even if you are prophetic, you still need to be humble enough to receive from God concerning your own life through the power of the prophetic.

1. Are you able to discern when the LORD is sending you help through a prophetic voice?

2. What are some reasons as to why David was unable to see himself in Nathan's parable?

3. Have you experienced seasons where you saw others' situations with clarity while simultaneously seeing yourself blurred? What do you believe attributed to that?

4. What parables (stories) has God employed in the past in the hopes of getting your attention?

How open have you been to Nathan's role? Sure, at the beginning of your pastorate, you may have welcomed Nathan's insight. You were excited and thrilled to be in a new leadership position. You were so humbled to be the pastor and entrusted with the church. You saw Nathan as a help, an advisor, and somewhat of a guardrail.

1. In what ways have you changed as you became more and more aware of the liberty your role provides?

2. How have you been stewarding the loyalty people give to you? Do you guard it or do you exploit it?

3. What happened when you learned how to cover up your poor choices independently?

4. *David, David, David.* What has being on the throne done to you?

COUCH *Conversations*

The biggest trick of the enemy is to pervert your view of God's protection. The concerns that you keep dismissing as correction are actually God's protection. Your sight can shift based on your height. The higher you go, the less clarity you may have. Somewhere along the way you may have started to believe that because you're on "the pulpit" you can no longer be positively impacted by the pew. Leader, I understand the magnitude of your flaws may be great, but despite your previous efforts, you cannot fix them by yourself. The beautiful thing is, you don't have to. You need to be open to God sending you help through a Nathan. Deal with your shame head-on. Stop hiding your flaws. Process how you got here, then do the work to transcend. Stop pushing Nathan away. The breakthrough you need is on the other side of your willingness to let in a prophetic light.

1. Have you distanced yourself from some voices that you now realize were sent from God? If so, why?

2. Have you misinterpreted inquisition for disrespect and opinions for dishonor? If so, what root brought that forth?

BONUS TASK

In response to the message brought to him by the Prophet, David repented. His fellowship and peace with God was restored and he was able to continue to lead. However, if God had not sent a prophetic word to awaken him to himself, his life and works could have ended in 2 Samuel 11. But by the grace of God, the prophetic word was given and received, which ushered David to arrive at Psalm 51.

Use the following lines to write your own Psalm 51.

_____

_____

_____

_____

_____

_____

_____

_____

_____

_____

_____

_____

_____

_____

_____

_____

_____

_____

_____

_____

_____

_____

_____

_____

_____

_____

_____

_____

_____

_____

TOP 3 TAKE-AWAYS

TAKE

a deep

BREATH

| | | | | | | |

SESSION SIX

The Supernatural Power of Rest

Leadership demands the need for a multiplicity of tools such as wisdom, discipline, discernment, and effective communication, just to name a few. However, in my counsel with leaders, I have found that absent from their arsenal is a tool critical to their success, as well as the success of that in which they lead. That tool is called REST. Rest is defined as ceasing work or movement in order to relax, refresh, or restore oneself; to recover strength. When most people hear or read the word rest, it often has a passive connotation. However, rest is a verb, an action word. Though at times rest can feel passive, what it produces is powerfully active. It is from that understanding that I have coined the phrase, *The Supernatural Power of Rest*.

1. How well are you resting?

2. What are some current obstacles that you feel are preventing you from living a rested lifestyle?

BIBLE STUDY: REST

A Psalm of David. The LORD is my Shepherd [to feed, to guide and to shield me], I shall not want. He lets me lie down in green pastures; He leads me beside the still and quiet waters. He refreshes and restores my soul (life).

PSALM 23:1-3a

In Session Four, we explored the duality of our personal lives versus our callings. Thus, we are embracing that though at times we are under shepherds, we are also still sheep. This session is designed for the soul of the sheep, in order to preserve the under shepherd. Only from a sheep space can you utter the words, "The Lord is my Shepherd."

Engage this session acknowledging, as David did in Psalm 23, that I, too, need to be fed. I, too, need to be guided. And, I, too, need to be shielded. Sheep leader, the Lord wants to shepherd you through this session. It is the Lord's intention to show you a portion of your life that could be lacking. What you may not have known is that rest has the supernatural power to guide. Rest has the supernatural power to feed. Rest can be a canopy of shielded protection. Therefore, you, Leader, cannot afford to cast another vision, host another conference, or hire another team member until you have submitted to the supernatural power of rest.

1. How can rest feed?

2. How can rest guide?

3. How can rest shield?

4. What are the benefits of stillness?

It's interesting that in some translations of Psalm 23 it uses the word make or maketh. Make means to intentionally cause something to come about. God will often make us rest because we neglect to see the necessity of rest.

1. Have things been occurring in your life that have been loud beckonings for you to rest? List a few below.

2. How have you been using noise as a panacea for your soul?

3. How have you been using the busyness of your schedule as a bandage for some of your gaping soul wounds?

4. What fears arise when you think of answering the call to rest?

5. How can you staff your life to support your need for rest?

COUCH
Conversations

Rest is God's way of ensuring our vitality and longevity. For those in leadership capacities, you cannot afford to just rest or replenish once. It must be a consistent discipline that you begin to see value in. While you are serving the world, your soul still matters to God. It is God's ultimate desire that many people are healed through your gifts poured out, however, God also has the power to keep you whole along the journey. Was Jesus, in many ways, a wounded healer? Yes! We do, however, need to grapple with whether, theologically, we are called to do the same. We may need to finally release the emotional weights God never intended for us to carry. Rest is a major way to lay every false burden down.

There are multiple layers to rest: spiritual rest, physical rest, intellectual rest, and emotional rest.

SPIRITUAL REST

It is impossible to rest our physical bodies if our spirits are ill at ease. Have you ever had something really bother or weigh on your spirit? Even after wrestling with that thing all day long, you still can't shake it off. So you take a good hot shower, get into a bed with fresh clean sheets, and turn off the lights. Unfortunately, even though the environment is perfectly set, you still can't seem to fall off to sleep. If you've ever wondered why, it's because when your spirit is ill at ease, your body will follow suit. So God says primarily, "You must have rest for your spirit, before you can experience rest for your body." The greatest result of Sabbath resting is the opportunity for your spirit to rest in the presence of God.

1. What practices can you implement to increase your times of spiritual rest?

PHYSICAL REST

The Sabbath is never a day to allow ourselves to be pushed, especially by our own false guilt or others' expectations, into an activity. If we are not able to rest one day a week, it means we're taking ourselves far too seriously. Leader, you're not that important. The job will continue to move forward. The church will still hold service. The usher board will still be able to usher. Everything will be okay if you take some time away. Previous generations perpetuated the notion, "I can't take a day because they need me." And as a result, young adults were not properly groomed for the next generation, and many an endeavor, organization, and edifice have crumbled due to leaders' inability to properly gage when their presence is required, and when it can just momentarily expire.

2. What practices can you implement to increase your times of physical rest?

INTELLECTUAL REST

Intellectual rest is vital for those with analytical minds. We tend to be the most troubled when it comes to rest. In the silence of our Sabbath times, our minds can rest, lending the freedom to learn anew how best to use our minds to the glory of God. Ceasing from labor and resting our brains dispels the frenzied fear that drives our minds when we fall prey to the world's expectations for constant accomplishment. In addition, our intellectual rest gives us the courage to give up any senseless thinking or intellectual pride that might thwart God's promises.

3. What practices can you implement to increase your times of intellectual rest?

EMOTIONAL REST

Rest was the manner in which God decided to settle Elijah's emotions, organize Elijah's emotions, sort through Elijah's emotions, and strengthen Elijah's emotions. (See 1 Kings 19) Mind you all of this would be occurring not BY Elijah, but WITHIN Elijah, supernaturally, as he rested. But notice that not only did he rest but he was refueled after coming out of that rest, and this occurred not once but TWICE! Through this rest God not only restored Elijah from his previous battle, God also fueled Elijah for his future battle.

4. What practices can you implement to increase your times of emotional rest?

SESSION SIX

TOP 3 TAKE-AWAYS

TAKE
a deep
BREATH

Let's

TAKE ACTION!

| | | | | |

Healthy Leadership in Action

Leader, in the previous sessions we walked through many thought provoking conversations with the goal of assisting you in becoming emotionally well enough to carry out the assignments God has given you. In our final session, I will provide you with some actions items (what I've compiled as a suggested code of ethics) to maintain your own health and integrity, and that of the ministries you lead.

In addition to a compromised emotional well-being, another reason some Christian clergy are moving unethically, is because we don't have defined morals that govern how we carry out ministry. Despite having the Bible as our ultimate North Star, our many denominations, doctrines, and interpretations of our sacred text have lended to discourse among clergy about what is and is not acceptable. However, ethics is not an issue of doctrine, denomination, or interpretation. You can choose not to believe in The Holy Trinity, but if you don't believe in the dignity and worth of people, beyond being a good leader, it may be necessary to consider if you are a good human being. Ethics is simply about whether your existence does good in the world or causes harm.

1
SERVANTHOOD

Ministry servant leaders must consistently keep at the forefront that the Bible is clear that "The greatest among you shall be your servant." (Matthew 23:11) We are charged with the care and aid of those that follow our leadership, therefore those who carry greatness will show greatness, not in asserting dominance, but in a life of servanthood.

What challenges have you encountered living by upside down kingdom principles in a right side up world?

ⅰ ⅰ ⅰ ⅰ ⅰ ⅰ TAKE ACTION! ⅰ ⅰ ⅰ ⅰ ⅰ ⅰ

- As a ministry servant leader, how can you implement this principle?

- As a part of the Christian clergy community, how can you guard this principle?

2
DIGNITY AND WORTH OF ALL PEOPLE

Ministry servant leaders respect the inherent dignity and worth of all people. We are called to treat each person we encounter in a caring and respectful fashion. We are mindful that regardless of one's circumstances, socioeconomic status, cultural differences, or beliefs, people deserve to be treated with respect.

What group have you been challenged to treat with dignity and respect? What could be a possible root of your challenge?

ⲓ ⲓ ⲓ ⲓ ⲓ ⲓ **TAKE ACTION!** ⲓ ⲓ ⲓ ⲓ ⲓ ⲓ

- As a ministry servant leader, how can you implement this principle?

- As a part of the Christian clergy community, how can you guard this principle?

3
SOCIAL JUSTICE

Ministry servant leaders are called to exhibit an empathy and sensitivity to ethnically diverse populations and to assist and come alongside their efforts to combat oppression. We are tasked with the courage to take on issues of social injustice on behalf of those that are marginalized due to circumstances beyond their control.

What social injustices are you most passionate about? How can you offer solutions?

׀ ׀ ׀ ׀ ׀ ׀ ׀ TAKE ACTION! ׀ ׀ ׀ ׀ ׀ ׀ ׀

- As a ministry servant leader, how can you implement this principle?

- As a part of the Christian clergy community, how can you guard this principle?

4
SEXUAL RELATIONSHIPS

Ministry servant leaders should avoid sexual activity with those whom they are in authority over. There is a clear power dynamic that infringes on the ability for the relationship to be experienced by either party from an equal and sober place.

Have you ever been aware or involved in a sexual relationship that had a skewed power dynamic? If so, how did it impact the people involved, as well as the people surrounding those involved?

׀ ׀ ׀ ׀ ׀ ׀ TAKE ACTION! ׀ ׀ ׀ ׀ ׀ ׀

- As a ministry servant leader, how can you implement this principle?

- As a part of the Christian clergy community, how can you guard this principle?

5
CONFIDENTIALITY

Ministry servant leaders should possess the ability to honor and therefore keep private all information that is shared with them in confidence, or that their position may warrant them being aware of that is sensitive in nature. The clergy role must remain trustworthy and safe. Therefore, the keeping or management of privacy must be paramount. Confidentiality, under the banner of being a mandated reporter (which all licensed clergy are), should be broken only in the case of suicidal or homicidal ideation and any sexual occurrences with a minor or non consenting adult. In those instances, family, the intended victim, and/or the authorities should be notified immediately.

Have you ever broken someone's confidentiality or been accused of such? If so, how was the relationship impacted?

׀ ׀ ׀ ׀ ׀ ׀ **TAKE ACTION!** ׀ ׀ ׀ ׀ ׀ ׀

- As a ministry servant leader, how can you implement this principle?

- As a part of the Christian clergy community, how can you guard this principle?

6
ACCOUNTABILITY

Ministry servant leaders benefit from willingly submitting to accountability. As a metaphoric umbrella, accountability can be a layer of covering as well as protection. Accountability should flow in three directions, the benefit of having a pastor/spiritual leader, the support and sounding board that comes from trusted colleagues, as well as the humility that comes from being accountable to those you serve.

What thoughts or fears come to mind when considering being accountable to those you lead?

ıııııı TAKE ACTION! ıı ıııı

- As a ministry servant leader, how can you implement this principle?

- As a part of the Christian clergy community, how can you guard this principle?

7
CHARACTER

Ministry servant leaders should be principled, sincere, and fair. It should be our aim to choose the highest most Christ-like choice, even if that choice may be difficult or cause discomfort for ourselves or others. We choose to take responsibility for our actions without displacing. We are free of corruption and hypocrisy in speech and deed, in both public and private spaces.

What steps can you take to ensure that your private personhood is congruent with your public personhood?

, , , , , , TAKE ACTION! , , , , , ,

- As a ministry servant leader, how can you implement this principle?

- As a part of the Christian clergy community, how can you guard this principle?

8
EMOTIONAL HEALTH

Ministry servant leaders must keep at the forefront that "you can teach and preach out of what you know, but you can only lead out of who you are" {Pete Scazzero}. As emotions can impact decisions, how we manage the emotional components of who we are can make or break our leadership. Seeking out various forms of counseling can prove to be advantageous regarding any unaddressed soul wounds, as well as assisting with the maintenance of existing wellness.

What leadership decisions have you made under emotional duress that you regretted under sobriety?

ⅠⅠⅠⅠⅠⅠ TAKE ACTION! ⅠⅠⅠⅠⅠⅠ

- As a ministry servant leader, how can you implement this principle?

- As a part of the Christian clergy community, how can you guard this principle?

9
PHYSICAL HEALTH

Ministry servant leaders are cognizant that in many instances, they are the tool. There is significant physical exertion used in Ministry Moments, especially in teaching and preaching. Intentionality in getting weekly physical exercise is critical to ensuring endurance, stamina, as well as mental clarity. Movement is medicine.

What and when can you add to your daily regimen a minimum of 30 minutes of physical exercise?

ⅠⅠⅠⅠⅠⅠ **TAKE ACTION!** ⅠⅠⅠⅠⅠⅠ

- As a ministry servant leader, how can you implement this principle?

- As a part of the Christian clergy community, how can you guard this principle?

10
COMPETENCE

Ministry servant leaders should only operate within their current level of competency. We should pursue continuous higher education, and ministry development trainings, so that we can perform our duties at the highest level required. All senior ministry leaders should possess both a bachelors degree, as well as a Masters of Divinity or Biblical Studies degree.

How would you describe your past experiences within academic contexts? (Go all the way back to grade school.)

׀ ׀ ׀ ׀ ׀ ׀ TAKE ACTION! ׀ ׀ ׀ ׀ ׀ ׀

- As a ministry servant leader, how can you implement this principle?

- As a part of the Christian clergy community, how can you guard this principle?

I I I I I I

SESSION SEVEN

TOP 3 TAKE-AWAYS

THE FACILITATOR'S GUIDE

TAKE *a deep* BREATH

Greetings Facilitator!

When The Head Hurts Workbook is designed to aid leaders in healing the emotional dis-eases hindering them from living healthy lives and leading healthy churches.

Though this workbook is a journey intended to benefit the individual, many leaders may find the process easier to navigate with the support of others. This facilitator's guide will provide you with helpful tips to ensure healthy and safe group discussions.

Choosing to embark upon a journey of healing through facing dark, painful truths, admitting one's faults, tearing down faulty borders, and erecting sustainable boundaries requires bravery. It is equally courageous to offer yourself as a guide to those who desire to undergo this process.

Understand that your role as a facilitator through this book will provide you with sacred access into the souls of those God has chosen to under-shepherd His sheep. In your experience, you will witness the transformation and enlightenment of leaders. But you will also have a front-row view of their humanity, their tears, frustration, brutal honesty, denial, and regret, amongst many other things.

As you prepare in advance by reading the book "When The Head Hurts," familiarizing yourself with the activities and questions, and intentionally praying for the group you will lead, this guide will help you navigate each session.

HOW TO ENGAGE WITH THE GROUP

1. **Prepare the meeting space with prayer.** Whether you are meeting online or in person, it's vital that you pray for the space. Welcome

Holy Spirit to purify and charge the atmosphere and make it conducive for healing and breakthrough.

2. **Lean on God as you serve.** Much like the leaders you will help as you facilitate this workbook, you can not accomplish this task without God. Rely on His strength, wisdom, insight, and will as you engage with the group.

3. **Resist the temptation to pass judgment.** Seeing anointed authority figures in such a vulnerable state may be a shocking and eye-opening experience. Depending on how you view leaders, it may be challenging to hear their truth or see their brokenness. Resist the urge to see them as anything less than children of God seeking help. Remain loving, kind, empathetic, and compassionate. After all, many of them have refused to undergo this process due to fear. Don't cause hurt in a space intended to heal.

4. **Release it ALL to God.** After each session, be intentional about laying down the experience at Jesus' feet.

5. **Let God BE GOD!** Understand that every emotional issue or layer of brokenness won't be completely worked out during the session. Keep in mind that they will only be with you for an hour or so, but God never takes His eyes off them. If a leader seems resistant or closed, give them space. Do not push. Trust that God will help them to process and fully heal in His timing.

6. **Lead by example.** There may be moments where your transparency will be helpful for participants. Be willing to verbalize vulnerability by sharing examples from your own life journey. One caution... *Be intentional not to overshare so that attention isn't taken away from the attendees.*

BEFORE EACH SESSION

1. Read the corresponding chapter in the *When The Head Hurts* book.

2. Work through the workbook content before each session. If you are familiar with the material, you will be more comfortable facilitating the session.

GUIDELINES FOR FACILITATING THE SESSION

1. Open with prayer.

2. Ask for a volunteer to read the session summary pieces and bible study verses. Select different participants weekly.

3. Allow participants time to answer each question individually. Once everyone has answered, choose a way to share. Either allow them to share their answers with someone sitting near them or select 1-2 participants to share aloud with the entire group. Be sure to thank each participant for sharing, regardless of their responses.

4. Couch Conversations and reading the next chapter is homework. Begin each session (after session one) by discussing the Couch Conversations from the previous week. This is a great way to review before moving into new content and conversation.

HELPFUL TIPS FOR FIRST GROUP MEETING

1. Set guidelines and rules for the group discussion.

2. Ask participants to introduce themselves, giving their name, the amount of time they have served in their leadership role, and one

thing they hope to experience from taking this journey.

3. Facilitate icebreakers to help participants connect and feel more comfortable with each other.

4. Make sure that participants have the materials before class begins (*When The Head Hurts* Book + *When The Head Hurts* Workbook); communicate in a preparation email that they should read the Introduction and Chapter One of *When the Head Hurts* Book before attending the first group session.

5. Remember to emphasize the importance of completing the Couch Conversations on their own.

6. If the participants in the group haven't completed *When The Head Hurts* book prior to engaging this workbook, ensure they're reading one chapter at a time in between each workbook group session.

ABOUT THE AUTHOR

Dr. Khaalida Forbes, a native of New York, holds a Bachelor of Arts degree in Sociology from Virginia State University, both a Masters degree in Clinical Social Work as well as a Masters of Divinity degree from Howard University, and an earned Doctorate of Ministry degree in Prophetic Preaching for the 21st Century from United Theological Seminary.

Dr. Forbes, known as "The Change Architect", is a multi state licensed clinical therapist. She is the Founder and Chief Executive Officer of Khaalida Forbes Enterprises. This enterprise seeks to offer opportunities for transformation in the areas of mental, emotional, relational, and spiritual health.

Having worked with adults and adolescents for 25 years, Dr. Forbes has extensive experience treating various forms of emotional disturbance. Her therapeutic modality of choice is cognitive behavioral therapy, and her specialization is trauma therapy. Dr. Forbes has held leadership roles in various organizations geared toward emotional health advocacy, with an emphasis on reconciliation of families from various ethnic backgrounds. Her endeavors have taken her around the world (Italy, Egypt, Israel,

London), and she trains quarterly throughout the year to ensure that she is on the cutting edge of what is occurring in the mental health, and faith field, across the country.

It is not often that you come across a therapist and leader that can weave the clinical, practical, and spiritual in a way that the well adjusted as well as the acutely traumatized client can relate. Dr. Forbes does this with equal parts finesse and innate ability. She strives to empower people to believe that through competent and compassionate therapy they can be healed, restored, and see significant lasting changes in their lives.

To join Dr. Khaalida Forbes' community focused on emotional wholeness, scan the QR code below.

www.ingramcontent.com/pod-product-compliance
Lightning Source LLC
Chambersburg PA
CBHW041118120626
46547CB00019B/2755